STATION X

STATION X

H. L. Dennis
Illustrated by **Isabel Muñoz**

Collins

Chapter 1
Inside the code-breaking factory

What I am about to tell you is top-secret. Listen carefully and get ready to remember every **w**ord. I want you to join m**e** on a very important mission. **L**ives are at stake, and you might just be able to help save them. Are you up for the challenge? If you are, then you'd better get ready to trave**l**.

How far? I hear you asking. Well, the **d**istance is not really the important bit. It's the time. Because we are going to go backwards … through the decades … right back to 1938.

But you asked about the distance, and so now you know when we are going, I should tell you where. To a mansion. A beautiful h**o**use with high turrets and fancy stained-glass windows. And incredible things are going to happen there. Hold on tight. Take a breath and trust me. Because Bletchley Park Mansion, 1938, here we come.

You can open your eyes now. We're here! Quite a ride, don't you think? But look where we are. I told you it was fancy. This mansion has been owned by the Leon family for over 50 years. But times are changing. Not just for the Leons – for the country. For the whole world, in fact. Remember, it's 1938. And I'm afraid I have to tell

you that across the sea in Europe, storm clouds of terrible danger are gathering. Keep close. I'll do my very best to keep you safe.

It looks like we've arrived with perfect timing. The new owner of the marvellous mansion is here too. Despite the scary news from overseas, Captain Faulkner's excited about his new house. And who wouldn't be? It's got 27 bedrooms, a conservatory, a magnificent ballroom, a fabulous library and even a fountain spurting water out of an ornamental lake. Oh yes – and there are lots and lots of frogs!

OK – the frogs aren't why Captain Faulkner bought this mansion. But look, the frogs are everywhere, hopping in and out of the lake and leaping up and down the lawns. Watch out! You'll learn that Bletchley Park Mansion is about to be crammed full of secrets. Even the frogs might be hiding clues you should look out for.

Captain Faulkner has wonderful plans for the land here at Bletchley Park. But I've already warned you that times are changing. Watch very carefully, you might just be able to spot a rather official-looking man striding down the driveway. Admiral Sir Hugh Sinclair. He's from the government and is in charge of **MI6**. He's come to have a quiet chat with Captain Faulkner.

He's here to talk about war.

The enemy, called the **Axis powers**, are making plans to take over Europe. To keep those plans safe and secret, the enemy are writing their plans in code. I'm sure you know already that codes are a way of hiding information, so that only those who understand the code can read the messages.

The British government is really worried. They know they need a team of code crackers to break these codes; that way Britain and its allies can prepare for enemy attacks and fight back. There's already a code and **cypher** school based in London that trains code crackers. But it's nowhere near big enough and there aren't nearly enough code crackers. What the government actually wants is a large, secret base in the middle of the countryside. They plan to bring together a huge team of smart and creative individuals. They want these people to use puzzle-solving skills, not weapons, to fight. They will be a different type of soldier in this coming war.

It would be ideal if this secret base is away from any large cities, in case the enemy plans bombing raids. It needs, though, to be within easy travelling distance of London. Even better if it is about halfway between the top universities of Oxford and Cambridge.

Bletchley Park Mansion is perfect.

This is why Sir Hugh is here: to make a deal. The house will be prepared for secret use in this national emergency. And what happens in the mansion will be crucial. Bletchley will no longer just be a fancy country house with many bedrooms. It will become a secret code and cypher school. To help Britain get ready to take on the enemy. And to help the **Allies** win the war.

As we begin to explore the house, you need to be prepared. Only certain people can enter Bletchley Park Mansion now. That's government orders. What happens here must not be shared. There are fences topped with barbed wire, all around the grounds. If the enemy hear about the plan, they'll put an end to Bletchley and to the clever code crackers who are going to work here.

While we explore and learn more about codes, cyphers and secrets, you need to accept the ultimate top-secret mission. And the government has sent you a letter to explain. Here – take a read …

Dear code cracker,

Welcome to Bletchley Park Code and Cypher School. As you walk these grounds and meet those who work here, you must promise to keep alert at all times. Secrecy is vital. And there's a chance that not everyone you see here will be working to protect the country. You will have to use all you learn from these pages to keep an eye out for a **double agent**, who might be feeding information back to the enemy. But we will help you. All the information you need for the mission will be given to you as you explore. And remember: this is a national emergency. Lives are at stake! You must do your very best to pay attention at all times.

Good luck! We are depending on you.

Chapter 2
I welcome you to Station X

Let's get on with the mission!

If Bletchley Park Mansion is going to be a secret code and cypher school, I really think it needs a code name. Let's call it Station X.

Now, that name might confuse you. But the first thing the government has done is turn the mansion into something called a "listening station". The enemy are going to make their plans in code. When they want fellow enemy fighters to hear those plans, they're going to send the information through the air across radio waves. The enemy think they will be making secret broadcasts. But the British government has worked out how to tap into those radio waves and listen in. It means the Allies are going to hear the coded messages. And the enemy won't even know they've been stolen. It's very clever. In fact, it's totally brilliant!

The government has set up listening devices in the dingy attic space of the mansion. All the coded messages that are sent from enemy battleships and submarines, and all the communications used by the enemy armies, will be listened in to.

There are already smaller listening stations across the country. In Roman numerals, the number 10 is written as an X; it's a form of code. And Bletchley Park is the tenth listening station. So, messages from every other station will finally end up here. At Station X.

And look, here in the dusty attic of Station X, you can see the equipment we're using to listen in.

The listeners have to concentrate really hard. All they hear are jumbled messages. Mind the cobwebs and move in closer. Can you make sense of the noises you hear? No? I didn't think you'd be able to. Not yet at least. Because of the codes. It will be up to the code crackers to work out exactly what the messages mean. And when they do, people here at Bletchley will know what the enemy has planned.

Now, if we need code crackers, I think it's about time the government got the actual code and cypher school up and running. Let's see if we can find the person in charge of the military section at Bletchley. His name is Brigadier Tiltman. The best place to find him is in his office.

I expect you're thinking that the Brigadier's office is somewhere very serious-looking. Perhaps there's an enormous desk, with charts and maps pinned up on the wall. I'm very sorry to disappoint you. When the Leon family owned the mansion, Tiltman's office used to be a nursery. So even now, the walls are still covered in Peter Rabbit wallpaper. It's odd, don't you think, that so many life and death decisions are going to be made here, with Beatrix Potter characters watching on? But life is moving quickly, and there are more important things to do than redecorate. Like I said, there are code crackers to recruit.

You might be wondering what sort of person would make a good code cracker. Brigadier Tiltman has very clear ideas. And so does Commander Denniston. That's him over there, sorting through that huge pile of papers. Commander Denniston is in charge of recruitment, and he and Tiltman both know exactly what sort of recruits are needed here at Bletchley. People who don't just follow the crowd.

People who aren't afraid to give things a go. And, most important of all, people who are determined not to give up. Making mistakes is an important part of code cracking. It's how we learn. Breaking codes involves lots of trial and error. And the best bit is that everyone at Bletchley, from the most highly ranked officials like Brigadier Tiltman and Commander Denniston, to the youngest and most junior of recruits like you, is going to be given the chance to say what they think.

If you have an idea about how to solve a code, you must speak up! But you have to learn to listen to others, too. Because being a code cracker also means being part of a team. So, how exactly do people get selected for this incredibly special team?

The most unusual way to be chosen is via a crossword puzzle. A specially prepared crossword in the *Daily Telegraph* newspaper, to be precise. Puzzle lovers have to try and complete the puzzle in under 12 minutes. That's not long, is it? But if the puzzlers do this and all their answers are correct, then the team at Station X will send a special telegram. This is what it says:

POST OFFICE TELEGRAM

YOU ARE TO REPORT TO STATION X AT BLETCHLEY PARK, BUCKINGHAMSHIRE. YOUR POSTAL ADDRESS WILL BE BOX 111, C/O THE **FOREIGN OFFICE**. THAT IS ALL YOU NEED TO KNOW.

What a puzzling message. It might make people really nervous, but I bet it also makes them itch to know more.

Take a look at this crossword puzzle. The answers have been filled in but the clues are still below so that you can follow it. Can you organise the words into a sentence to give your own special message?

Across
2. not that
3. a bit
5. can't be shared
7. when something belongs
8. not me

Down
1. a special job
4. it means "to be"
6. the highest part of something

Some of the recruits arrive by train at Bletchley village station in the middle of the night. As the steam train pulls away into the darkness, these new recruits have to find the telephone box and phone the mansion. No one has a mobile phone, of course. They haven't been invented. The receptionist at the mansion answers the call with these simple words, "We've been expecting you."

Do you think this makes the recruits feel better or worse?

They've left their homes and families and many of them have travelled for days across the country. And they don't even know yet what kind of work for the war they will be involved in. Then, with their hearts hammering in their chests, they're led to an abandoned train carriage, just beside the train track.

Even before the recruits have spied the mansion through the trees surrounding it, they're interviewed about their ability to keep an important secret. You see, once they get to the mansion, they will have to sign a very important document. It's called the Official Secrets Act. Recruits sign a promise. Never, ever to speak of their work or tell anyone about their training.

What happens here at Bletchley will change the course of the war. But if the enemy hear about it, then Britain and all her Allies will be in serious danger.

Being good at crosswords isn't the only thing that might make you a good code cracker. Some people are chosen because they know lots of different languages. Others because they're very good at maths. But Tiltman and Denniston also know that playing games can make you good at solving problems. It can help you to never give up. They've decided that chess players should be part of their team.

I bet you'd like to meet some of these recruits. Look, there are two of the very best chess players the country has ever had. Stuart Milner-Barry and Hugh Alexander. They've been champion chess players since they were young.

STUART MILNER-BARRY

HUGH ALEXANDER

I wonder if Stuart's hand shook a little as he signed the special document promising to keep government secrets? I wonder if Hugh's stomach clenched with nerves at the thought of what might lie ahead here at Station X? But Tiltman and Denniston know both men will be good at cracking codes. Let's follow them inside the mansion and find out. Because now other recruits have arrived, it's about time you and I had the chance to properly explore.

Chapter 3
Hunting for important codes

As we re-enter the mansion, time has moved on a little. It's 1940 now, and that means the war is underway. It also means the mansion's packed with people. Workers with diamond-sharp minds, ready to help their country in its time of threat. So come quickly. I don't want you to get lost in the crowd.

To help you keep your bearings, I think it's a good idea to look at this blueprint of the mansion. Can you find the billiard room? That's a huge room used for playing a game a bit like snooker. What about the ballroom? This room has a shiny, polished wooden floor and a ceiling decorated with plasterwork flowers and swirls. I'm afraid there's not much time for billiards or dancing, though. We've got to get on with the serious business of the codes.

To help you with them, I thought now might be a good time to give you your very own codebook. The recruits here are learning lots about codes, so it's important you keep up. We want you to know about all sorts of ways of hiding information. The more you know about other codes and cyphers, the more everything happening here will make sense to you. Don't forget. You have a top-secret mission to complete. You have to find the double agent. I'm sure at least one of the codes in the codebook will help you with that.

Where's this codebook? Well, I'm afraid you have to break a code to find it. Cracking codes is all about taking things step by step. We know it's OK to make mistakes. Trial and error is how we learn.

So, let's get code cracking. Take a proper look at the blueprint of Bletchley Park Mansion's layout. To break the code, you have to go to each room numbered in the code. If you wanted to go to room 46, for example, you'd go to the ballroom.

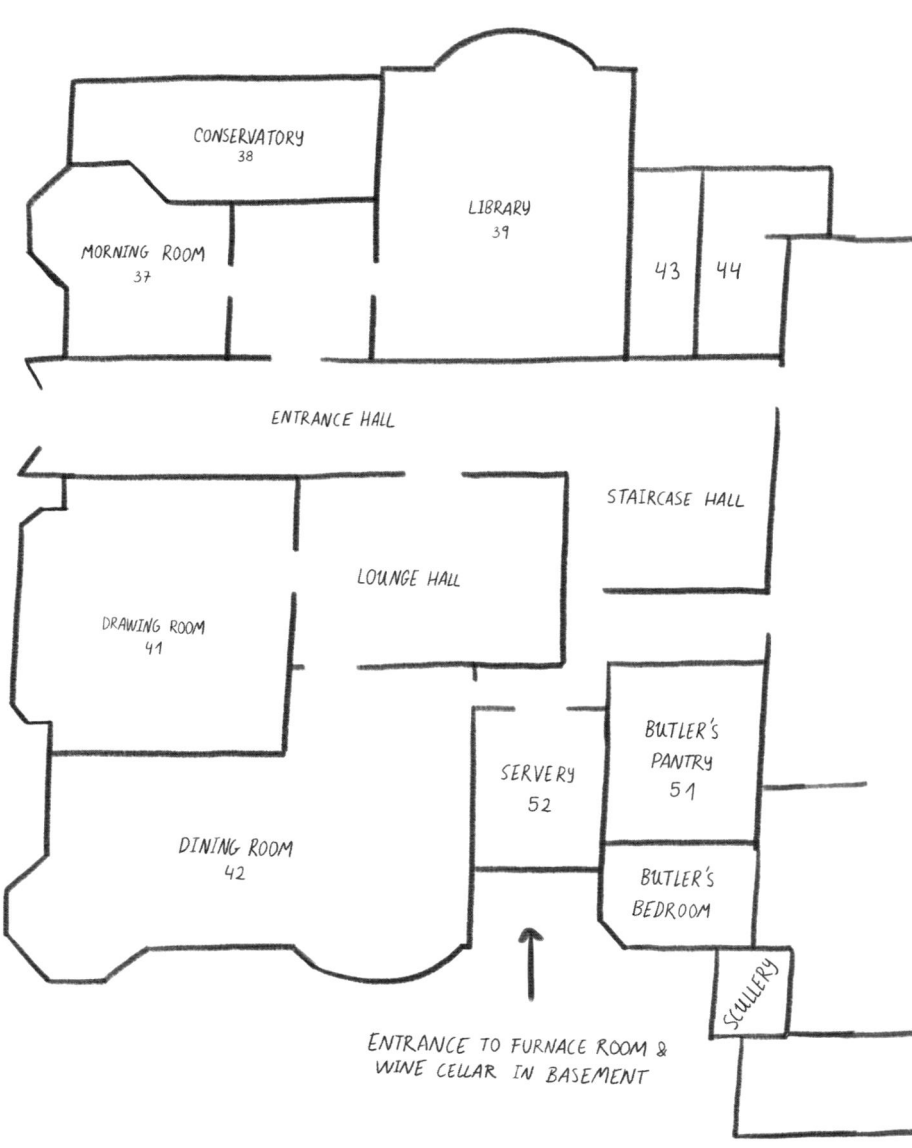

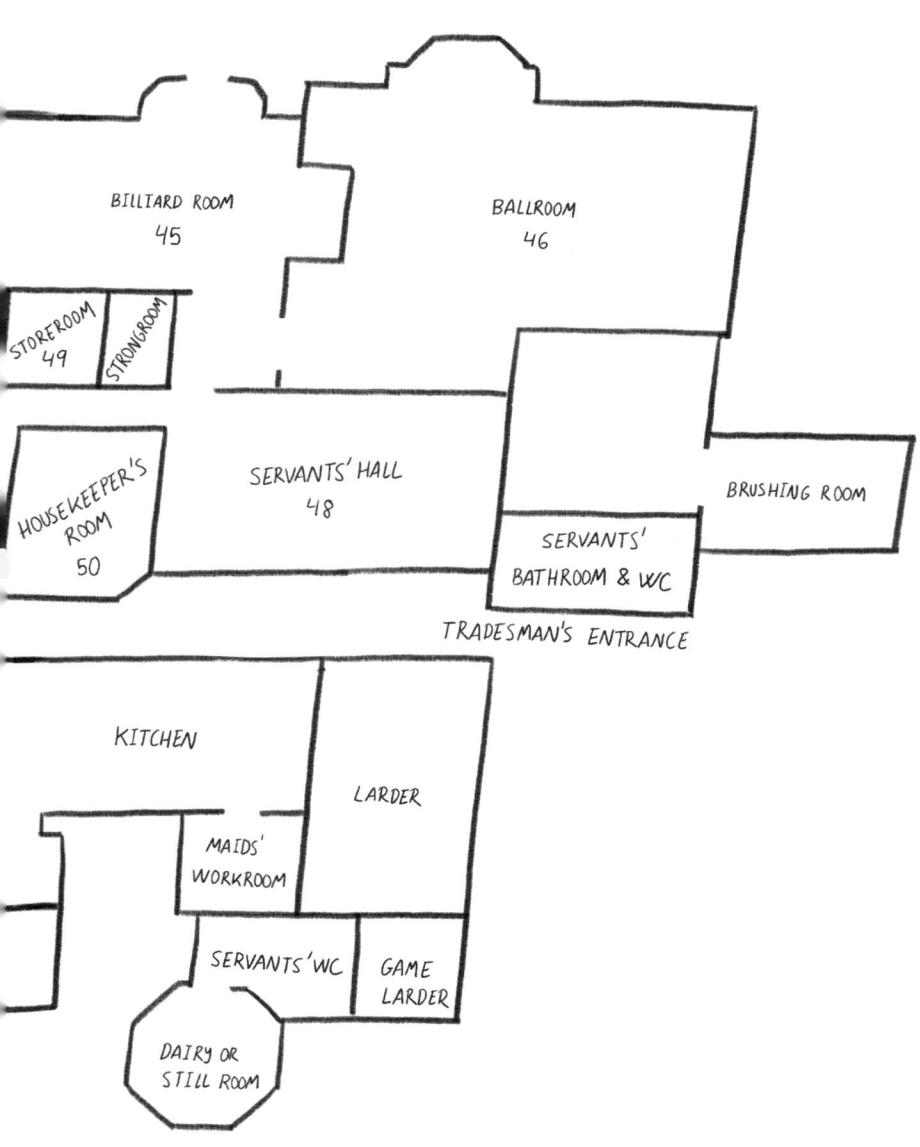

But that's not all. Next, you have to take the second number from inside the bracket. That gives you a letter from the room name you've just visited.

I'll help you with the first bit of the code: (52,1).

Can you find room 52? That's somewhere called the servery. When the house was still being used as a country mansion, this was the room where splendid meals were put together to be served.

Now, what about the number 1 in the bracket? The number 1 gives you the first letter of the room name. So, for servery, you take the letter "s".

Can you follow the code and find your codebook? Take it step by step, remember. And if you get really stuck, you can flip to the answers at the back of the book just to check where you should go.

Here's your code:

(52,1) (38,9) (46,5) (50,2) (48,6) (41,7) (49,4) (37,2) (45,10) (42,10)

Well done! You did it. I can see you're going to make an excellent code cracker. Now you're armed with your codebook. I suggest you keep it close to you at all times. Codes can be hidden everywhere.

Now you've got a proper sense of the layout of the mansion and you've seen how busy it's become, it's time we stepped outside again. Since we first arrived at Bletchley Park, you might notice things have changed a bit. The lake's still there, of course. And those frogs. Watch out! They're jumping through the flowers now.

This is a great time to tell you that even flowers can hold codes. They've been hiding secret messages for centuries. Take a look in your new codebook and see how each flower can represent something. Be sure to look at the meaning of a snapdragon. That's something you should definitely remember.

FLOWER CODE

SUNFLOWER
LOYALTY

ROSE
LOVE

PINK
YES

RHODODENDRON
STRENGTH

SNAPDRAGON
DECEPTION

IRIS
I SEND A MESSAGE

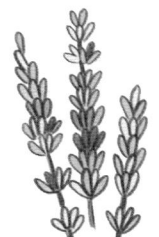
LAVENDER
DISTRUST

BEGONIA
BEWARE

DAISY
INNOCENCE

While we're walking through the grounds, checking out the flowers and avoiding the frogs, I want you to notice the change I was talking about. The place is so busy now. Just look at all the tatty wooden huts that have suddenly appeared around the grounds.

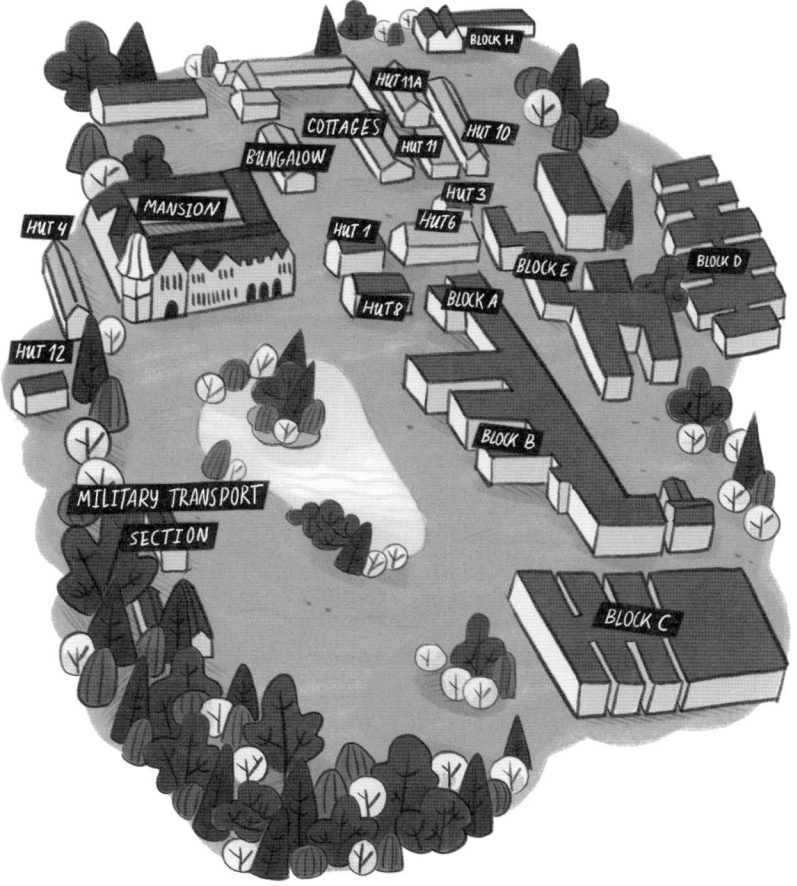

They look just like garden sheds. I wonder if you can work out what is happening in those.

But we have to wait a bit before we explore those, because first I want to take you just beyond the mansion. We're going across the courtyard, to the small line of connected houses next to the stables. We call this place "the Cottage". It's time to step inside so we can properly investigate.

Chapter 4
Reporting for duty

The Cottage is full of people battling with codes and, as we make our way inside, it's time to meet one of Bletchley Park's chief cryptographers. "Cryptographer" is a special word for code cracker. And this code cracker is one of the best there's ever been. His name is Alfred Dillwyn Knox. But everyone calls him Dilly.

DILLY KNOX

He's that man there – the very tall one with the wild, black hair and thick, heavy glasses. He's worked for the government as a cryptographer for years. But Dilly has been interested in codes since he was even younger than you. He once wrote to the writer of the Sherlock Holmes stories, a man called Arthur Conan Doyle, and told him there was a mistake in one of the codes in his detective stories!

Dilly is very clever. He learnt about ancient classic stories when he was at the University of Cambridge. For part of his work there, he used to study precious, crumbling papyrus, which is what Egyptians used to write on before paper. He spent so many hours concentrating on the tiny, ancient marks that he damaged his eyesight. But Dilly's mind is still really quick and some say he has a bit of a quick temper too … so we'd better be quiet as we watch him work.

If he does spot us, there's a tiny chance he won't remember later. Dilly's terribly forgetful. He even forgot to ask two of his brothers to his own wedding. It's because Dilly's mind is so often focused fully on his work. And his work is so important. At the moment, he's deciphering some naval codes. They're messages that have been sent from enemy ships. Dilly is in the middle of breaking a code sent by Italian warships. Once the code is broken, the plans of the Italian Navy will be sent on to the Allies' soldiers. The Allies will know where the enemy ships are. That's why what happens here at Bletchley is so important, you see. Dilly really is a genius.

But I don't want you to get the idea that Dilly does all this work on his own. Code cracking relies on teamwork. And Dilly doesn't work alone in the Cottage: he has lots of people who help him. In fact, just over there at the desk by the window is Dilly's assistant, Mavis Batey. She's hard at work, too.

MAVIS BATEY

Mavis studied German when she was younger, and she planned one day to become a nurse. Nursing would have involved a lot of training. Yet as soon as war broke out, Mavis knew she wanted to help straight away. She had no time now for medical training and she was desperate to use the skills she already had. She spoke to someone at the Foreign Office. They asked her lots of questions and tried to work out how good she would be at keeping secrets. She must have really impressed them with her answers.

At first, Mavis thought she was going to be sent off to become a spy. But instead, she was asked to do something very unusual. Mavis had to buy a copy of *The Times* newspaper every day. Her job was to check for enemy messages. The government thought that perhaps secret agents were planting codes in adverts or letters that the enemy paid to have printed in the newspaper. (I told you that codes truly can be hidden anywhere.) Mavis was so good at her job that the government knew she would work brilliantly at Bletchley. So, they brought her here to be Dilly's assistant. I think Mavis is a genius, too!

Mavis has been working with Dilly on breaking codes sent by the enemy and they've been using a system called "rodding". This involves the code crackers using massive grids called "rod squares" which list rows and rows of letters. You can see some spread across the table there. Don't worry if they look incredibly confusing – that's because they are.

The team use these rod squares to try and figure out how the letters have been swapped around by the enemy to write their cypher. The enemy changes the way they swap the letters every single day so there's no time to waste trying to find the right rod square to make each message readable.

Dilly has told everyone that as soon as they hit a dead-end and the rod square looks like it's not going to help them decipher the message, they should abandon it and choose another square. For three months, they've failed and failed to find the right cypher for each day's message. Something about the system just wasn't making sense. Until Mavis had a breakthrough.

Mavis hates giving up on anything. A few weeks ago, fired up by her own intuition and the inkling that the team were abandoning each rod square too soon, she decided to press on with the one she was using. An inconsistency of letters she'd found made it look certain this particular rod square was wrong. Everyone else believed she should give up. But Mavis just wouldn't stop. Persevering meant disobeying orders. Yet this brave decision meant Mavis found a way of making the rod square work, even though it looked as if there were glitches at the very beginning! Her determination to keep going means even more enemy plans have been deciphered. In the battles to come, attacks by enemy ships will be thwarted because of the information passed on to the Allied forces – from the team in the Cottage. Thank goodness Mavis was so bold. She wanted to do something important to help the war effort. And now she really is.

Before we leave Dilly and Mavis, it's a good time for you to take a look at your codebook. Sailors on ships have been using coded messages for centuries. There's a special kind of ship code called semaphore.

Semaphore works so well, it isn't just used at sea; you can use it on land, too. Once you know how it works, that is.

Give yourself a bit of time to study your codebook. Can you see how each different way of holding the flags is equal to a letter? And don't worry. The code works just as well if you haven't got flags. You can just use your arms.

What do you think? Got the hang of it yet? Because once you know how to wave your arms to represent letters, you're all set to send coded messages to anyone who can see you. But of course, you need a code breaker who can read the message you're sending. So why don't we pop over to those garden sheds that have sprung up all around the grounds? Perhaps there are some other code crackers there waiting to meet us.

It's finally time to check out the secret huts of Bletchley Park.

Chapter 5
Let's check out the strange huts

Now you're inside, can you see that the huts are actually bigger than they look from the outside? Long, aren't they? And do you notice how there are rooms off both sides of the passageway? Still, they're rather ramshackle, and not at all posh like the mansion. See how the windows are totally plain, with mesh on the outside to stop people peering in. No pretty stained glass here. And at night, those inside have to bring down the shutters because of the blackout. Any lights at all in the darkness could give away Bletchley's location to the enemy who might be flying in fighter planes overhead. This means no houses or places of work are allowed to have lights showing. If we were based in the village, you might hear the blackout warden shouting, "Turn that light out." But here at Station X, everyone knows the rules. And the simple, dim, yellow glow everyone works by comes from neon ceiling lights covered by thick green shades.

You might expect the code cracking to stop at night. It doesn't. The code breakers work in shifts. All night. All day. So be careful as you walk through the rooms. The floor squeaks and we don't want to disturb anyone while they concentrate.

Can you see how there are lots of people working at basic rickety desks? Some of the tables are covered with maps. The codes being broken back in the Cottage and in some of the other huts reveal where enemy ships are. People in this hut are finding the position of the ships on the maps. They're making notes on a blackboard propped on that easel.

All the codes and locations are checked in this hut. Then all the notes and code solutions are stored in those huge filing cabinets that run down the length of the far wall.

I should apologise about the smell. It's the fumes from the leaky coal-burning stove down there in the corner. Not that the stove does a very good job of keeping anyone warm in the winter. If you look carefully, you'll see that lots of the code crackers are wearing mittens. But it's even worse in the summer. The huts get suffocatingly hot and stuffy.

Oh, watch out! Not just the frog, but can you see someone hurrying in our direction armed with a broom handle? She's going to use it to push a tray of messages down a long wooden chute that connects this hut to the one next door. Code crackers do everything they can to save time. They need to act on the messages they decipher before the enemy changes their plans.

Oh, no: another disturbance. There's someone at the door. It's a motorbike courier. He's ridden through the night at breakneck speed, in a terrible storm. He's got a bundle of coded messages from another listening station. And he needs the "third uncle" to see them.

I haven't explained about the uncles yet. There are four of them. They're actually called "wicked uncles". This might sound mean but it's because they've been fighting so hard to get extra money for Bletchley to make sure the code cracking can continue. Some people in government have moaned about their nagging and that's why they've got the nickname "wicked". This hasn't stopped the uncles doing what they know is right and a few weeks ago, they were really daring. They wrote directly to the Prime Minister, Winston Churchill, bypassing the normal chain of command and pleaded with him to give Bletchley more money to keep solving codes. You've met two of the uncles already: Hugh Alexander and Stuart Milner-Barry. Now it's time to meet uncle number three: Gordon Welchman.

Welchman studied at the University of Cambridge and he's a totally brilliant mathematician. He helped choose lots of the workers here.

When people first started looking at enemy messages, Welchman realised it would be helpful to focus on where enemy messages were being sent from and where they were being sent to, not just the messages themselves.

He looked for patterns connected to times and locations. This way of studying the movement of the messages was called "traffic analysis". Looking for patterns in the "message traffic" is helping the team guess things like if the enemy troops are about to move on to somewhere new. Remember, the enemy don't know Bletchley are stealing the messages. They think they are secret!

Can you see how quickly everyone is sorting the messages, looking for patterns, and making sure that not a minute is lost? Let's go back to the bundle of messages delivered just now by motorbike. There's code breaking to do. Once the code is broken, the messages won't even be in English. They'll be in a different language: German, or Italian perhaps. Can you see that team of people sitting round that enormous desk at the other end of the hut? They're working on translations. Codes – to German – to English. It's a complicated, multi-stage business.

But not all codes have several stages. Some just substitute letters for shapes, like the semaphore you learnt earlier. If you want a little breather from all this frantic work around you, why not have a look at your codebook and check out another substitution cypher. It's called the Tic Tac Toe cypher.

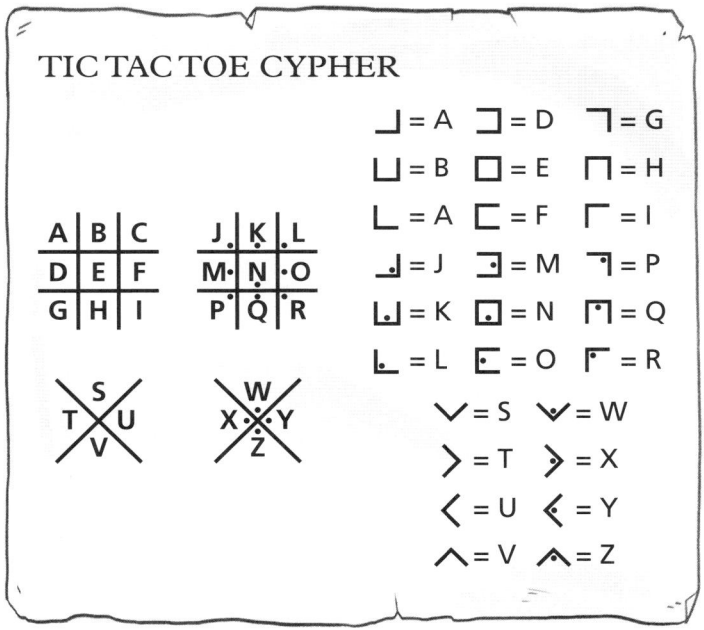

Can you decipher this coded message?

The letters have been substituted for symbols which show sections of a grid. It's a really ancient cypher and has been used for hundreds of years. Can you write your own secret message using Tic Tac Toe, before we head off to meet some other code crackers?

You've already met brilliant mathematicians and incredible chess players. You've met a man who spent so long studying ancient papyrus he strained his eyes and another who works in a Peter Rabbit decorated office. But you won't believe who we're going to meet next!

Chapter 6
Broken dreams and broken codes

We'll have to race through the rain to get to Hut 4. All the huts have numbers tacked beside the doors. The huts look the same from the outside, but each one is dealing with different groups of messages. The code crackers must never gossip about what happens inside each hut. Those who work in Hut 3 never share secrets with those from Hut 6. It's all part of the way things are organised.

Someone who really likes things well organised is the person I want you to meet. Here, shake off the rain and say hello to Pamela Rose. You might be wondering what Pamela did before the war which made her so organised.

Chess player, perhaps? Mathematician? But Pamela was neither of these. In fact, I bet you'll never guess what job she had. Pamela was an actress. Just like codes, code crackers can be found in all sorts of places.

PAMELA ROSE

Pamela's story is one of broken dreams and real bravery. Her brother is missing in action. That means that he was fighting as a soldier and no one's quite sure what's happened to him. Pamela's incredibly worried and she's also incredibly sad. Several of her friends have already been killed in the fighting. She was offered a part in a play, but Pamela is determined to do her bit to help defeat the enemy instead. So, she's using her brilliant organisational skills fantastically here.

Pamela sorts the index system in Hut 4. All the clues and answers must be put safely where people can find them and check them if they need to.

You remember those massive filing cabinets I showed you? Well, they're packed full of secrets. Who knew that being tidy and organised could be so useful. Because having everything in the right place is a really vital part of code cracking. Make one slip up with just one letter in a code, and you get a completely incorrect message. Misfile a message in the wrong cabinet and the thread of a secret could be broken. Lives could be lost.

People have always known that having things in the right place is important when sending codes. In fact, if you check out the next page in your codebook, you'll see a code that relies completely on where things are. It's a very old method of secret writing called the scytale code. It's when a strip of paper is wrapped around a long baton or rod. The message is then written along the length of the paper on the rod. But when the piece of paper is unrolled, the letters are all scrambled.

SCYTALE MACHINE

You can only read the message again by rewrapping the strip around another cylinder the same size as the original rod, and putting everything back in the right place. What a clever form of coding! I bet Pamela is excellent at this.

Someone else who might have been good at this type of code is Jean Campbell-Harris. Jean knows a lot about ranks, positions and organisation. In fact, in later life she will be known as Lady Jean or Baroness Trumpington. Jean's mother was a very rich American; her father a major. The family did lose lots of money before the war but prior to life here, working in a hut, Jean had experience of an exceptionally grand life. She went to boarding school, and then finishing school in France. This was a place where rich girls learnt all the skills they would need to be a lady. Sounds rather impressive, doesn't it? But Jean hated it!

Jean's father knew she wanted to live an exciting life. But Jean feared all she would get to do was sit at home all day. Her time at finishing school taught her things she would need to know when she mixed in **high society**, but it also helped her get very good at languages, including French and German. Jean's father arranged for her to meet someone from Bletchley, and Jean was given the chance to work here. She works

JEAN CAMPBELL

incredibly hard, and if you peep over there now, you can see she is changing some of those coded messages from German to English. Jean is a translator; breaking the codes is just one part of the job. Turning the deciphered code into a language we can read comes next.

All of the work here at Bletchley fits together like pieces of a puzzle. All the pieces of the puzzle are important. And all the people, too. The code crackers. The translators. Those who file the messages. They're all part of this incredible secret mission.

And as the war rages on, and time moves forward, you should know that there are several thousand people working here at Station X now! And nearly three-quarters of them are women. Some of them, like Jean, are from very wealthy backgrounds. But some of them are from much more humble homes. The work being done by a couple of those women we're going to focus on next is about to change the progress of the whole war!

Chapter 7
"Geese who never cackle"

As we dash off towards the next hut, make sure you notice that poster tacked to the wall. It's warning you to be careful about what you say to others. Remember – you can't tell anyone what you've seen in the hut we've just left. Someone who overhears you could be collecting information for the enemy. (Don't forget your top-secret mission is to look out for a double agent!)

The Prime Minister, Winston Churchill, calls the workers at Bletchley "Geese who never cackle". He's so proud of their ability to keep secrets.

Sharing what you've heard can be dangerous. But listening carefully is crucial. Do you remember the motorbike courier we saw earlier? Some of the messages he brought to Bletchley couldn't have got here at all if people hadn't been listening very carefully. You'll remember there was a listening station in the attic here at the start of the war. Now, because time has moved on and the war has intensified, listening stations have sprung up across the country. There are many more than ten now. The stations are staffed by people listening constantly to overhear enemy plans. The bundle of messages delivered today are being deciphered by Welchman's team. They are being translated by Jean. But they were overheard by a young woman called Betty Gilbert.

Betty's life before the war was very different to Welchman's; she didn't go to university, and she used to work in a shoe factory. Her life was also very different to Jean's; she lived in a very small house in Northamptonshire with no electricity and no bathroom and she even had to share a bed with her mum. We know that all the jobs here at Bletchley are important, but we need to remember that the work stretches out of here beyond the fences. As we hurry onward across the grounds, think of the life beyond the barbed wire we can see glinting in the moonlight; Betty's job is one of many that is vital to the work at Station X. If what happens at Bletchley is like a puzzle, then what happens beyond the fence is like links in a chain. One link is the delivery of the messages by the courier we saw arriving on his motorbike. But the very first link depends on people like Betty.

Betty overhears Morse code messages. Some of the messages that are picked up by Betty's listening station are spoken messages. But some sound just like knocking noises.

BETTY GILBERT

These noises are a substitution cypher too. A series of short knocks and long knocks that stand for letters of the alphabet. You can even write down the sounds – dots for the short sounds and dashes for the long ones. Take a look at your codebook and see how it works. And make sure to check this book for messages written in Morse code, just in case there are clues hidden about that double agent you're hunting.

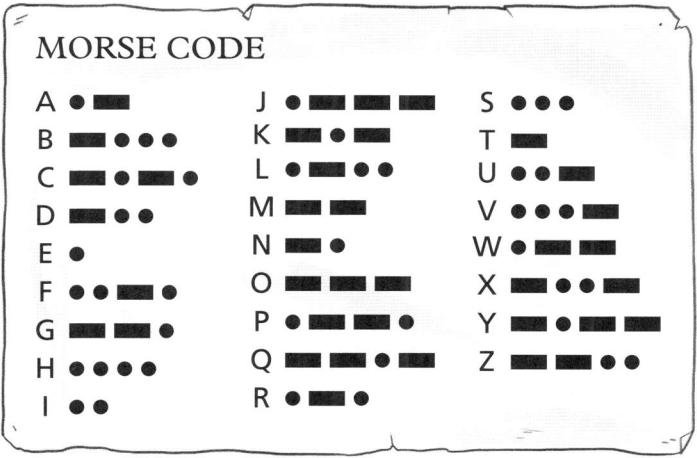

Betty's job is difficult. When you listen in to Morse code, you have to train your ear hard to hear it properly. Concentration is key. But we're going to have to concentrate really hard now. We've finally made it to Hut 8, and I should warn you that the work in this hut is some of the most complicated of all the work you'll see here at Bletchley. It's OK because the work is in very safe hands. The hands of someone called Joan Clarke. And if you keep extra quiet, we can watch her work.

Joan went to the University of Cambridge. We've already met Gordon Welchman, who also studied there. In fact, Welchman used to be Joan's teacher. Joan worked extremely hard at university and proved to all her teachers she was really clever. But she wasn't given a full degree. Before the war, Cambridge wouldn't give degrees to women. As you know now, over three-quarters of the people working here at Bletchley are women, so the rule at Cambridge was unfair and discriminated against female students.

Welchman knew Joan's brain was just as sharp and quick as a man's. So, he recruited her to work here at Bletchley as part of the **Ultra** intelligence project. That means Joan helps decipher messages sent using enigma machines.

Have you ever heard the word "enigma"? It tells us something is mysterious or difficult to understand. And the enemy are using enigma machines to make their most important messages to each other scrambled, muddled and therefore mysterious before they send them.

The mysterious enigma machines are at the heart of what is happening at Bletchley.

The rainstorm we raced through may have lifted. The motorbike courier might now be riding away from Bletchley into the light of morning. But I have to warn you that the storm clouds of war in Europe and across the world are getting fuller and heavier every day. The years are clicking on. As we moved from 1940 into 1941, attacks on the UK and her Allies have grown more intense. London and other cities like Liverpool and Coventry have suffered terrible bombing raids called the Blitz. That's why what's happening in Hut 8 is more important than ever.

It's finally time for enigma!

··· ·· / ━ ···· · / ··━· ·━·· ━━━ ·━━ · ·━· / ···· · / ·━━ · ·━ ·━· ···

Chapter 8
Winding the wheels of code

The enigma machine used by the enemy is stored in a simple wooden box. It looks like a typewriter or computer keyboard. Above the keyboard are three rows of lights on the lid. Each light has a letter printed on it. The code sender presses a letter on the keyboard. This makes a letter on the rows above light up. The lit-up letter is never the same as the letter pressed. Here, watch Joan as she shows you.

She presses letter A on the keyboard, but the lit-up letter is a G. So, in the code, the letter A will be replaced by the letter G. But how does the machine know which letter to light?

Well, firstly because there's something called a plugboard at the front of the machine. It's got lots of holes. (You can think of them like modern charging points for mobile phones.) The holes are labelled A to Z too. The first thing the code sender does is plug a wire from one hole into another one. They do this with lots of wires. It looks very messy when all the wires are plugged in.

Have you ever heard an adult say, "You've got your wires crossed"? This phrase comes from when old-fashioned telephone receptionists worked with plugboards like this, connecting one phone to another so people could talk to each other. If the receptionist made a mistake and mixed up the wires, people heard the wrong messages.

The phrase also works for the enigma machine because the wires being crossed over each other here muddle the message system too; but this time on purpose. When Joan presses a letter, the machine "thinks" she's pressing a different one.

That's stage one.

Next, can you see the three wheels, or rotors, behind the keyboard? Each wheel has 26 possible positions. The code sender sets the position of each wheel, and this also changes which letter the machine "thinks" has been pressed.

That's stage two.

So, to break the code, all we have to do is work out which wire and wheel settings the enigma machine used today. Then we'll know which lit-up letter has been swapped for which real one. Simple.

But here's the problem: those wires and wheels would give us about 159 million, million, million possible combinations! How on earth can Joan and the workers in Hut 8 possibly work out which letter stands for what? It would take forever!

To start with, the code crackers make "cribs". In cryptography, a crib means a "best guess".

You know how when you do a problem in maths, you should try and estimate the answer first? Well, cribs work like that. The code crackers use what they know about where the message came from to try and guess what it could say.

By this stage of the war, the code crackers have learnt from past solutions that messages sent from certain enemy locations often talk about rain or storms. They can therefore guess predictable words like "weather report" might be near the start of the message. Then they look for patterns of letters that might fit these words. But that's not enough.

Joan might use a "pinch" to help her. Pinches are codebooks that have been captured from the enemy. Enemy soldiers write down the settings of the wheels and wires they use each day. Looking in a "pinch" could be really helpful. In fact, one of the best code breaks that has already happened here at Bletchley was because a lazy member of the enemy didn't change the enigma machine settings every day at midnight with the care he was supposed to. It's likely he just banged the lid of the machine down and let the rotors slip a few places.

This meant that every day the settings were really close to the ones used the day before. The code crackers here used cribs and pinches to help them work out the settings he'd used. And because he didn't change the settings carefully enough, Station X workers could read enemy codes easily for days!

But if pinches and cribs and mistakes by the enemy aren't enough, then who can help now? The fourth uncle, that's who. And it's about time you met him: Alan Turing.

Turing will later be known as the father of computer science. The work he does here at Bletchley helps lead to the invention of modern computers. But for the moment Turing is called something else by Joan and those he works with: "The Prof". It's short for Professor, because everyone knows Turing is very, very clever!

ALAN TURING

Stuart Milner-Barry, the chess player we met earlier, says Turing always surprises him by thinking in such an original way. This means some of the things Turing does could seem a little unusual. He chains his mug to the radiator, for example, to stop other people like Joan or Stuart walking off with it. And, talking of chains, the chain on Turing's bicycle is broken. But instead of mending it, he's worked out how many times the bike wheels go around before the chain falls off. He simply dismounts just in time to reattach the chain, then carries on cycling. It's certainly original!

Speaking of things going around and around, we really should get back to talking about the enigma machine. What is Turing going to do about those 159 million, million, million combinations of wires and rotating wheels? I'll tell you what he's done. He's developed a code-breaking machine called the Bombe!

Welchman has helped Turing make the Bombe even better, but you should cover your ears because when the Bombe is working, it is incredibly loud! Let's hurry across to the next hut and see.

Look here: filling nearly the whole wall of Hut 11 is the Bombe. It has rows and rows of drums with letters on. Each drum represents a different position of a wheel in the enigma machine. And there are loads of wires plugged in at the back of the machine too. In fact, the Bombe works like lots of enigma machines all fixed together.

Joan and Turing start the machine by feeding in a bit of code they've worked on from their cribs and pinches. Then the drums begin to spin automatically. That's what's making the noise. The Bombe is testing every combination of wires and wheels, working faster than a human can think to find the settings the enemy enigma machine was using today. It's like the very first computer.

Oh, listen. It's suddenly quiet. The drums have stopped spinning. The Bombe has found today's enigma machine settings. Now Joan can set the wires and wheels on her own enigma machine to this combination. Next, she'll type in the full coded message. And the keyboard letters will light up to show the original message in normal language which we call "plaintext". Then all the team will have to do is translate the plaintext message from German to English. Perfect!

After seeing all this, you might be in the mood to make your own code machine using spinning wheels. It won't be as big as the Bombe. But it will be an excellent code wheel machine just the same. Check out your codebook to see.

CYPHER WHEEL

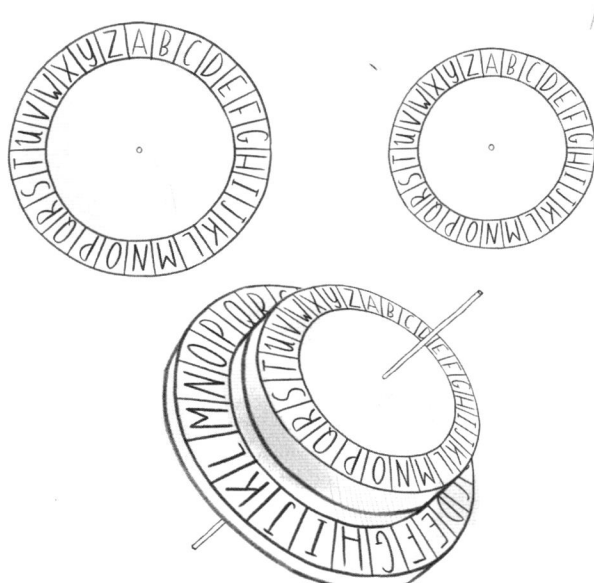

This cypher wheel uses a system called the Caesar Shift method.

1. Trace or scan these wheels.
2. Cut them out.
3. Attach the small wheel on top of the big wheel with a paper fastener.
4. Spin the wheel to let each letter find a partner in the larger wheel.
5. Use these new letters to write your message!

When you've done that, it's important that you see that Alan Turing couldn't have developed the Bombe without the work of others, first. And I don't just mean the others here at Bletchley. At the start of the war, Polish cryptographers had got much further than the British or French teams at working out how the enigma system worked. The Polish had even managed to reconstruct an enigma machine. Polish mathematicians Jerzy Różycki, Henryk Zyglaski and Marian Rejewski made major breakthroughs with deciphering the code system, and Turing learnt from their discoveries. He owes them lots of gratitude and so do all the Allies whose lives are being saved by the code solving happening at Bletchley.

Code cracking can often be like a relay race. Różycki, Zyglaski and Rejewski completed the first leg of the relay. Then they passed the baton on to Turing, and to all those we've met who are working so hard here at Station X to crack the code. And talking of relay races, who on earth is that racing past the door? We'd better leave Joan and Alan to their work and step back outside to check.

Chapter 9
Fun, food and free time at the fortress of secrets

It's Mavis, Dilly Knox's assistant from over in the Cottage. I wonder where she's going in such a hurry. Perhaps she's racing to meet someone important who's just arrived at Station X. Winston Churchill came here in September 1941. And some of the army generals have popped in too. They come to meet those who are working behind the scenes to help those who are fighting on the **front line**.

Mavis does seem to be heading in the direction of the sentry boxes at the back gate. Anyone who comes in has to pass the sentries who are on watch. But maybe Mavis is just going home to her billet, having worked through the night. Billet means a place where people stay. They don't sleep here at the mansion, you see. Unless, of course, they are working so hard and so long on the code that they fall asleep at their desks. Instead, they stay in family homes in the nearby villages. The government has made every household let them know how many rooms they have. You can't turn down a worker from Bletchley if you have space. And the rent for these places is taken straight from the wages paid by Bletchley Park, and given to the landlord directly.

Many of the workers don't live in family homes, though. Pamela, who's lived on her own since she left school and wasn't really keen to share a room, refuses to live in any sort of billet. She rents a caravan in a nearby field! But other code crackers live together in another mansion called Woburn Abbey. That's 16 kilometres from here. It sounds very grand, but actually, it's rather awful! There's no hot water, the drains are often blocked and the food is terrible. Breakfast is just left-overs from the night before.

And remember: no one can tell anyone outside Bletchley Park what they are up to inside. If anyone asks where you go all day, you give only one answer: "Work". If anyone asks what you do there, you give only one answer: "Work". That's it. You can't say anything else to anyone. Family. Friends. People who own your billet. Keeping the secret must be exhausting.

That's why many of the workers choose to spend their spare time at Station X along with other people who are keeping the same secret. After all, there's the library to borrow books from and the lake to boat on, or swim in, if it's warm enough. It's far too cold today. Even the frogs are scurrying off to hibernate. In fact, the lake has frozen over. Some brave people are skating on it, though. I think I can spot Jean gliding as fast as she can on her blades. I hope the ice doesn't break. The skaters are taking a risk, but they deal with risk and things breaking all day, every day, as they try to crack the codes. So, skating is a good way to let off steam. Look at them go! I'm afraid I don't recognise all of them because they're skating so fast.

If the skaters are worn out afterwards, they can always book to use the fancy bathroom in the mansion. You're allowed one slot every fortnight and Joan can't believe how beautiful and relaxing the baths are. She's never known anything so luxurious.

Look over there. Someone else we know. Although I don't think she's going skating.

It's Pamela. She's off to join some of her friends at the Bletchley Park Drama Club. Putting on a play together helps the code crackers switch off from the stress of work but also helps them all get even better at working as a team. A vital member of the team is Pamela's friend Jim who's helping backstage. I've heard that today is Jim's birthday. Maybe they'll celebrate with a dinner party. Although the last one held at Station X wasn't that successful.

Food is rationed due to the war which means you have to take a special book of vouchers with you to the food shop, and you are only allowed certain items each week. Even then, the shop often runs out of things you need so shopkeepers substitute food we usually eat for rather unusual alternatives. At least being a code cracker helps you be creative. Our code crackers know all about substitution cyphers so they substitute real eggs with powdered eggs from a tin to try and make cakes. Instead of bananas, they substitute mashed parsnips mixed up with banana essence and call this mock banana. I've heard that none of this actually tastes that great but at least they're trying. But you'd better be especially prepared if they ask if you want ice cream. For many years during the war, all ice cream has been banned because its ingredients are in short supply. Yet the code crackers have an ingenious solution. They attach carrots to sticks to make them look like ice-lollies. I'm not sure everyone agrees that this is the tastiest substitution!

Trial and error. Taking risks. Being creative. It's all part of being a good code cracker. That, and being part of a team who now and then sit down to dinner together. So, if we are going to end with a dinner, then let's make sure the table is carefully prepared. Grab that tablecloth. And perhaps check your codebook, just in case even the table is hiding a code for us. Oh, and one final tip. However hungry you are after all this time looking around, whatever you do, don't eat the banana cake served with ice cream!

Chapter 10
A cracking conclusion to the code

Well done for keeping up with me as we dashed through time, exploring Bletchley. And good job avoiding all those frogs.

Can you hear that bell clanging? There seems to be lots of excitement. Quick! Let's hurry to find out what's happening. It's May 1945 now, and I think that bell is ringing because of very good news. The war in Europe has ended! And what you saw here at Station X was a major part of making that happen. No wonder the code crackers are so happy!

As we watch them now, exhausted but relieved, they don't look like soldiers, do they? But they really have been fighting a war. A battle to find out what the enemy had planned, and to stop them.

I've heard that the Supreme Allied Commander, General Eisenhower, thinks the work at Bletchley helped to shorten the war considerably. He's a very important man and will go on to become President of the United States in just about eight years from now. He believes, as do lots of other people, that hundreds and thousands of lives have been saved because of the work done by these very ordinary-looking people. Pamela, the actress; Betty, the factory worker; Dilly, the man who studied so hard he hurt his eyes; Joan, the woman who studied so hard but was not given a full degree. The chess players, the mathematicians, the organisers, the motorbike couriers and the geniuses who worked day and night to make sense of the code have all played their part. Their work was not done with guns and tanks but with pencils and paper, a massive amount of teamwork and an awful lot of brainpower!

Code cracking really is like a superpower. And you've done such an excellent job of understanding the codes. Maybe you can use them now to send secret messages to your friends. You can tell them that codes can be hidden absolutely anywhere.

Before we travel back to the future, we should check you've discovered every code hidden within these pages. Because if we learn nothing else from these wonderful people at Bletchley, we should learn never to give up, however tricky the problem we are facing.

I wonder if, for example, you worked out why I kept asking you to look out for frogs. Did you notice that each frog we saw had speckles on its back? The speckles were substitutes for letters. One speckle equals letter A; two speckles equals letter B; three speckles letter C and so on. Go back and check on those frogs and see if you can find a message about that double agent you were looking for. And there's a Morse code message about the double agent hidden somewhere in these pages too. I really hope you've found the double agent! Another thing we should learn from those at Bletchley is that being a trustworthy member of a team is absolutely vital.

And I hope too that you've found the other secret messages hidden for you. Did you spot the letters written in bold at the start of chapter 1? What do these letters say? And what about in the chapter headings – did you see the flower hanging from each letter? Collect the letters and read the message hidden there!

What about the semaphore message hidden for you? Did you work this out too?

There's also one final code to wrap up this adventure. And you need to have read this whole book to solve it. Check out the last page in your codebook to see how it works.

BOOK CODE

Can you break the book code?

Look at these numbers.

(23;2;4)

(2;5;1)

(44;16;4)

(65;17;5)

(34;5;1)

(6;20;2)

(19;10;9)

Take the first number in each bracket to find the page number from this book.

Take the second number in each bracket to find the line of text on that page.

Take the final number in the bracket to find the word in the line.

Can you break the final code to find your final message?

Before we head off, the team of code crackers at Bletchley have something else to give you. They've been very impressed with your effort!

We must get ready to travel in time once more. We'll hang around at Bletchley for a while, but I think we need to plunge back into our own place in history. So, hold on tight. Take a breath. And trust me. Because, Bletchley Park Mansion, present day, here we come.

Epilogue

We're here! Quite a ride, don't you think? It's often easier to go forward in time when we've learnt so much about the past. We're still at Bletchley, and you might be surprised to see that it looks a bit like it did when we were there in the 1940s. There's the mansion, look. And the huts. And there are also lots of extra things to see because Bletchley Park is now a museum. People can come here and, just like you, they can learn all about what happened in the Second World War.

If you've been paying attention, you might be worried about how that can be happening. We watched all the workers sign the Official Secrets Act.

They promised not to tell. Ever! And for a long time after the war, no one did. In fact, the mansion didn't look like this at all for a while. It was taken over by the Post Office and used as a training centre for engineers. And many of the huts you see now are replicas of the ones we saw back in the 1940s.

Most of the original huts were pulled down. The Bombe machines were dismantled, and all the papers and the messages were burnt on enormous bonfires so the secrets and codes could never be shared. For the years straight after the war, people worried that there might be a new enemy who would use enigma machines to send messages. It would be a terrible idea to let the world know we'd worked out how to read these messages.

Everyone kept the secret, which meant none of the brave workers at Bletchley could ever properly celebrate what they'd done. They couldn't even tell their families and friends what they'd got up to. People sometimes asked them what they did in the war. And because you've read this book, you should know what they had to say: "Work".

It wasn't until 1974 that someone finally thought it was a good idea to share what happened at Bletchley Park and he wrote a book. Frederick Winterbotham had been involved with Bletchley Park at the start of the war, although he wasn't a code cracker. Instead, he worked for MI6 and managed reports which gave details about the information revealed every time a code was broken.

Winterbotham claimed that in 1972 a journalist knocked on his front door and asked what he knew about wartime ultra-secret information. Winterbotham maintained he went to the Ministry of Defence and argued that, if anyone was going to reveal the secret about what happened at Bletchley, it should be someone who worked for the government and not a journalist. Apparently, the Ministry of Defence agreed he could write the book as long as he promised not to reveal any information about how exactly the codes were cracked. Lots of the workers at Bletchley were horrified. They wouldn't read the book, or talk about it. But as the years passed, the need to keep the secret began to crumble. And so did the mansion.

In the 1990s, the Bletchley Park Trust was formed to try and save the building and turn it into the museum we see now. The house was in a terrible state. The shiny polished floor of the ballroom was coming up. The carved and decorated ceilings were coming down. But teamwork, brainpower and determination not to give up saved Bletchley Park. It means that past code crackers have been able to talk about their work at last – if they want to. It means that people who worked at Station X in the war could meet each other and finally celebrate all that they achieved. And it means that people like you and me can learn from their example and the important part in history they all played together.

Thankfully, the bonfires that burnt the messages and papers did not destroy the memory of what happened at Station X. The secrets have risen again, like a phoenix from the ashes to finally be shared. You know the power of these secrets now. And you can help pass the story on, so it is never, ever forgotten. Perhaps *that* should be your final top-secret mission!

Glossary

Allies in the Second World War, the Allies (or Allied powers) were a group of countries who were fighting together to stop the enemy. The Allied countries included the UK, the US, the Soviet Union, China, France and Poland. Membership of the Allies varied across the years of the war and after 1942 the Allies became known as the United Nations.

Axis powers the main enemy of the Allied powers in the Second World War. These nations included Germany, Italy and Japan.

cypher a form of secret writing. While codes replace whole words with other words or groups of letters, cyphers swap individual letters or sounds with symbols. Or, the order of the letters in a message is changed. Cypher is often spelt "cipher" now, although during the Second World War it was spelt "cypher". Most people use the words "code" and "cypher" to mean the same thing. And Morse code is actually technically a cypher. But you don't need to worry about that. Just remember cyphers hold secrets.

double agent someone who pretends to be working for one country but is actually spying for another country

Foreign Office the part of the government responsible for trying to keep the country safe from international threat. During the Second World War, the Foreign Office managed all the discussions between countries. And it ran all the secret departments used to help in the fight against the enemy. Bletchley Park was one of these places.

front line the part of the army that is closest to the enemy and involved in the physical act of fighting

high society people who come from rich and important families

MI6 the UK's foreign intelligence agency responsible for espionage. This is the practice of using spies (typically by governments) to collect political or military information.

Ultra British code name (from June 1941) for all the high-grade signal intelligence. This was the information sent that was thought to have been put together using the most complicated coding systems. This included all the information sent from enigma machines.

Answers to the codes

Check all your answers to the codes built into the book. Remember to try and work them out first before you look!

CHAPTER HEADING CODE

Find all the letters that have a daisy hanging from them in the chapter headings. We know a daisy means "innocence" from looking at the flower code. So, we know we can trust this message. All the letters with daisies can be used to spell out this message: SUPERB WORK

CODE HIDDEN IN THE INTRODUCTION OF CHAPTER ONE

Spot the letters written in **bold**. They spell out the message: WELL DONE

THE FROG CODE

Look for the speckles on the back of the frogs. Substitute these for letters. 1 = A; 2 = B; 3 = C, and so on. Collect all ten frogs to get the message: FIND ICE MAN. That should lead you to search beside the frozen lake to find your double agent.

CROSSWORD PUZZLE (page 13)

Take the words from the puzzle and arrange them to give a message. It reads: YOU ARE PART OF THIS TOP SECRET MISSION

WHERE'S YOUR CODEBOOK? (page 22)

(52,1) (38,9) (46,5) (50,2) (48,6) (41,7) (49,4) (37,2) (45,10) (42,10)

Use the numbers to discover the rooms needed. Then, within the name of the rooms, find the letters.

Servery (S); Conservatory (T); Ballroom (R); Housekeeper's Room (O); Servant's Hall (N); Drawing Room (G); Storeroom (R); Morning Room (O); Billiard Room (O); Dining Room (M)

Discover the codebook in the: STRONGROOM

SEMAPHORE FLAG SIGNALS (page 33)

Collect all the semaphore flags in chapter 4 through to and including chapter 10 to make the message: A SECRET

TIC TAC TOE CYPHER (page 41)

Use the letter substitutions to reveal that the message written in Tic Tac Toe says:

DON'T FORGET TO LOOK FOR THE DOUBLE AGENT

MORSE CODE (pages 53 and 55)

... .. / − .... . / ..−. .−.. −− .−− . .−. /
.... . / .−− . .− .−. ...

Check against the Morse code to read the message: SEE THE FLOWER HE WEARS.

This clue leads you to the flower code. Did you guess what kind of flower the double agent is wearing? It's a snapdragon flower (deception).

TABLECLOTH CODE (page 72)

Find the letters peeping through the holes which give us the message: GREAT WORK

WHO IS THE DOUBLE AGENT?

Combine several code solutions to find the answer. The frog code asked us to "find ice man". Then the Morse code asked us to "see the flower he wears". Finally, the flower code tells us that the snapdragon means "deception". This is a word which means lying, false, not true, or trick.

So, the man beside the frozen lake wearing a snapdragon is our double agent! Fabulous work if you found him. That is a real multi-stage code to solve where you had to put lots of pieces of the puzzle together. Great work!

BOOK CODE

Collect all the words from across the book to uncover your final code message. It says: Excellent. You have completed your top-secret mission!

Book talk questions

What kind of person makes a good code breaker?

Can you describe the different ways a message can be turned into a code?

Which code breaking method did you like the most?

In what ways did people contribute to the war effort outside of the battlefield?

What was the role of the four uncles at Bletchley Park?

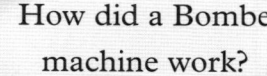

How did a Bombe machine work?

If you worked at Bletchley Park, would you be able to keep their secrets?

Did you crack all the codes hidden in the book? Which one was your favourite?

How different would code breaking be using today's technology?

Can you think of a new way to code a message?

Ask the author

What inspired you to write *Station X*?

My modern code-cracking adventure series *Secret Breakers* is based at Bletchley Park, so I jumped at the chance to share some of the intriguing real stories about what happened there in the Second World War.

H. L. Dennis

What was your favourite part of this book to write?

I loved thinking up codes for readers to find and hiding them in the text.

Would you have been able to keep what happened at Bletchley Park a secret?

I'm very chatty so I would have found it extremely hard. But I understand why the secret had to be kept so I would have tried my absolute best.

Are there any spy books or films that you like?

I love any books or films that include codes! I'm a fan of both *National Treasure* films. They don't include spies but do centre around mysteries connected to real places and real historical puzzles.

What role would you take if you worked at Bletchley Park?
I'm not very good at languages, but I am extremely good at sticking with a problem and not giving up. I would have loved to have been Alan Turing's assistant and work alongside Joan Clarke.

Are there any other resources you would recommend to someone interested in Second World War history?
Bletchley Park itself has a fascinating website. If you're lucky enough to get the chance to visit the museum there, you should definitely go!

How do you think code breaking has influenced popular culture in the years since the Second World War?
Action films like *Indiana Jones* and *Mission: Impossible* make excellent use of people's love of puzzles, and of course we use codes all the time when we have to remember computer passwords and pin numbers.

Who is your favourite code breaker?
Pamela Rose. I love the idea of an actress turned code breaker who lives in a caravan!

Published by Collins
An imprint of HarperCollins*Publishers*

The News Building
1 London Bridge Street
London SE1 9GF
UK

Macken House
39/40 Mayor Street Upper
Dublin 1
D01 C9W8
Ireland

Text © Helen Dennis 2026
Design and illustrations © HarperCollins*Publishers* Limited 2026

10 9 8 7 6 5 4 3 2 1

ISBN 978-0-00-878470-6

All rights reserved. No part of this publication may be reproduced, stored in a retrieval system, or transmitted in any form by any means, electronic, mechanical, photocopying, recording or otherwise, without the prior written permission of the Publisher or a licence permitting restricted copying in the United Kingdom issued by the Copyright Licensing Agency Ltd, 5th Floor, Shackleton House, 4 Battle Bridge Lane, London SE1 2HX.

Without limiting the exclusive rights of any author, contributor or the publisher of this publication, any unauthorised use of this publication to train generative artificial intelligence (AI) technologies is expressly prohibited. HarperCollins also exercise their rights under Article 4(3) of the Digital Single Market Directive 2019/790 and expressly reserve this publication from the text and data mining exception.

British Library Cataloguing-in-Publication Data

A catalogue record for this publication is available from the British Library.

Author: H. L. Dennis
Illustrator: Isabel Muñoz (Bright Agency)
Publisher: Laura White
Commissioning editor: Holly Woolnough
Development editor: Zoë Clarke
Product manager: Holly Woolnough
Content editor: Selin Akca
Copyeditor: Sally Byford

Proofreader: Catherine Dakin
Reviewer: Lisa Davis
Fact checker: Sasha Morton
Cover designer: Sarah Finan
Internal designer: 2Hoots Publishing Services Ltd
Typesetter: David Jimenez
Production controller: Sophie Waeland

Collins would like to thank the teachers and children at Grange Primary School, Southwark, for being part of the development of Big Cat Read On.

Printed in the UK

MIX
Paper | Supporting responsible forestry
FSC® C006032

Made with responsibly sourced paper and vegetable ink

Scan to see how we are reducing our environmental impact.

Get the latest Collins Big Cat news at
collins.co.uk/collinsbigcat